HELLBOY ™

SEED *of* DESTRUCTION

D1406310

HELLBOY ™

SEED *of* DESTRUCTION

by
MIKE MIGNOLA

Script by
JOHN BYRNE

Miniseries colors by
MARK CHIARELLO

Cover colors by
DAVE STEWART

Short-story colors by
MATTHEW HOLLINGSWORTH

Published by Dark Horse Comics
10956 SE Main Street
Milwaukie, OR 97222

First edition: October 1994
Second edition: June 1997
ISBN: 1-56971-316-2

INTRODUCTION

by ROBERT BLOCH

F SOME-
ONE HAD
TOLD ME
FIFTY YEARS AGO THAT
I'd ever write the introduction to a collection
of comics, I'd have told him he was crazy, and that *I*
would have to be crazy in order to do so.

Back then I was writing short stories for the pulp
magazines. Neither the publications nor the material I
sent them was a major contribution to the status of
American literature, but by virtue of it I could at least call
myself a writer. Today I probably could have made the
same claim — and gotten more critical and media
attention — if I'd just gone around spraying out *graffiti*.
Nevertheless, even though I lacked such opportunities, I
was a published writer. Some of my colleagues, equally
proud of their status, were less satisfied with their
incomes. Under various pseudonyms they moonlighted,
turning out scripts and story lines for the comic books.
But this was not something one talked about in polite
society, nor spoke of in private. Even in those days there
were limits to admitting one's indiscretions; anyone might
proclaim himself a born-again Christian, but few would
admit to being a burn-again Satanist.

And comic books, to some, were satanic. They were
gross, sleazy vehicles of violence, and their creators were
the kind of people who gave child-molesting a bad name.

So thought Dr. Frederick Wertham, a psychiatrist
who launched an attack on these dime-store demons. The
odd thing is that this same Dr. Wertham, a few years
thereafter, was quite critically impressed by my first novel,
The Scarf, and in ensuing correspondence the good doctor
and I traded opinions about comic violence, just as though
neither of us was aware of the murder and mayhem I
perpetrated on the printed page.

But things have changed over the past
half-century — things like comics, and myself.
And at least some of them — the comics —
have improved.

Back then it was easy to trace the roots
of the story comics to the pulp magazines,
from which many series characters
were transported and transplanted to
the paneled pages. Artwork showed
the influence of newspaper comic
strips, cartoons, pulp magazine
illustration, and the films of
the era. Much of what

those early comics offered was derivative, and some of it
did, at least in part, justify the criticism of well-
meaning do-gooders who feared their children would
become read-badders.

And the comics were an influence, no doubt about it.
Youngsters who came under that influence grew up to
become influential themselves, as writers, artists, filmmakers.

Today, the influenced have become the influential, so
that cause and effect have done a flip-flop. Now the
comics are the innovators; newspaper art copies
their style, and other forms of graphic art and illustration
frequently adopt their techniques. And the whole
"language" of modern film and television seems quite
obviously translated from comics in the form of jump-
cuts, enormous head shots, rapidly changing POV, and a
dozen other innovations which determine emphasis and
pacing — and careful editing.

All of this has been generally accepted under the
convenient label of "pop art," but there are indications that
talented artists, writers, and editors are starting to stretch
that label. Not satisfied with endless (and frequently, mind-
less) repetitions of the mixture as before, they are reaching
out to broader concepts, bolder methods of reaching a
more adult readership, new ways to tell old tales.

Hellboy is a brilliant example of how to elevate the
comic of the future to a higher literary level while achieving
a higher pitch of excitement. Its story line combines
traditional concepts with modern frames of reference, the
whole being swept along by a *virtuoso* treatment of dazzling
artistic effects.

As in any experimental venture there are, of course,
minor flaws. "Yeah, right" was not a sarcastic phrase used
in 1944, nor was anyone or anything characterized as
"Looney Tunes."

But these are quibbles — mere flyspecks on the dome
of the Sistine Chapel. The total effect of *Hellboy* is that of
a true work of art — original and innovative and exciting.
Again and again you'll find panels and pages which
display a sophisticated and sometimes deliberately
satirized awareness of classic modes and content. The
product of superb talents, they could be framed
and stand forth on their own. Striking use of color
enhances their effect and complements the impact
of plot and scripting.

This is far from the "pop art" of the
Andy Warhol world or the inane imagery of
the drug culture. The creative approach
found in *Hellboy* is a newly evolving art
form of its own, addressed and
attuned to today.

Besides, it's a killer read!

For Jack Kirby, H. P. Lovecraft,
my lovely wife Christine, and
the amazing Elmer Newton.

CHAPTER ONE

Journal of 1st Sgt.
George Whitman, USA
12/23/44
East Bromwich, England.

We've been here for two days now and it isn't getting any better. All of the men are jittery in this place. Maybe if it had a name. Maybe if the people in the village would even talk about it. But they won't.

Not even telling them there could be a crack team of Nazi commandos lurking about somewheres gets anything out of them. They just look at you like Nazis are maybe the last thing in the world they need to worry about.

If that were true, we wouldn't be here.

Okay--this is what we think we know: Hitler has sent some kind of team to England. I called them commandos, but there's a trio of people from the British Paranormal Society who say they're more than that. They say the Germans are some kind of spook squad. That the krauts are here to perform some kind of spell or something. Summon monsters. Raise the dead.

Yeah, right.

But whatever it is, it's got the top brass worried enough to send a special Ranger unit to look into it. And the Torch of Liberty is here with us. Funny to see him standing there, having a cup of joe with the rest of the guys. I'm more used to seeing him jumping around in newsreels, fighting some cockamamie Nazi menace.

Seems like an O.K. guy, though. And he believes this whole business. He says his own sources confirm the Nazis are in the final stages of something called "Project Ragna Rok".

I don't think our Limey friends were too thrilled to learn it took the Torch's word to make us believe them.

There's three of them:

Professor Malcolm Frost, from Blackfriar's College, stateside.

Trevor Bruttenholm (pronounced "Broom") who's some kind of paranormal Whiz Kid.

And Lady Cynthia Eden-Jones, who's supposed to be England's top medium.

And in charge of this whole Looney Toon party is me, a guy who'd never even heard the word "paranormal" before a week ago.

Anyway, two days camped out in this holiday camp and so far nothing. No spooks. No monsters. No Nazis.

But Lady Cynthia says it's going to happen here. And it's going to happen tonight.

Only thing is, she can't say just what "it" is.

WELL, "BROOM"? YOUR *REPUTATION* GOT US HERE, BUT SO FAR ALL WE'RE DOING IS *FREEZING* OUR DAINTY LITTLE *BUTTS* OFF.

SERGEANT, I HAVE SPENT THE LAST NINE YEARS *STUDYING* THIS PLACE, TRYING TO DISCOVER WHAT HAPPENED HERE LONG AGO THAT WAS SO HORRIBLE IT *ERASED* ALL WILLINGNESS OF THE LOCALS TO EVEN *DISCUSS* THE MATTER.

"WHEN LADY CYNTHIA TOLD ME THE *DISTURBANCE* SHE HAD SENSED IN THE ETHER WAS *CENTERED* HERE..."

NO. WAIT.

THERE IS... *ANOTHER*... A SECOND CENTER.

"BUT IT IS *NORTH* OF HERE. FAR NORTH..."

"I SENSE... *COLD*, AND *WATER*. IT IS A TINY *ISLAND* JUST OFF THE *SCOTTISH COAST*..."

CHAINED IN HEAVEN ARE THEY. SEVEN IS THEIR NUMBER. BRED IN DEPTHS OF OCEAN, NEITHER MALE NOR FEMALE ARE THEY. THEY ARE AS THE HOWLING WIND, WHICH KNOWETH NOT MERCY, WHICH KNOWETH NOT PITY.

WELL?

THIS BLEAK PLACE SEEMS REMARKABLY *UNCHANGED* FOR A *MIRACLE* TO HAVE OCCURRED HERE.

SPARE ME YOUR *SARCASM,* VON KRUPT.

SARCASM? MY SARCASM IS THE VERY *LEAST* OF YOUR WORRIES, *SORCER-ER.* YOU PROMISED THE *FUEHRER* A *MIRACLE.* SOMETHING WHICH WOULD *REVERSE* THE *COURSE* OF THIS WAR AND ENSURE THE *VIC-TORY* OF THE *REICH.*

HERR *HITLER* DOES NOT TAKE *KINDLY* TO *FAILURE.*

I HAVE NOT FAILED, VON KRUPT.

I HAVE SET IN MOTION EVENTS WHICH CANNOT NOW BE *REVERSED* OR *UNDONE.*

I PROMISED HERR HITLER A MIRACLE.

"I HAVE MADE ONE."

HO-LEE...

SHOOT IT! KILL IT! IT'S A DEMON COME FROM HELL TO DESTROY US ALL!

IT... DOESN'T LOOK TOO DANGEROUS TO ME, PROFESSOR.

IT LOOKS... LIKE A LITTLE BOY...!

...HELLBOY...

"THE EXPEDITION. THE THREE CAVENDISH BOYS. SVEN OLAFSEN, THE RENOWNED ARCTIC EXPLORER. ME.

"YES. I REMEMBER. NINETEEN DAYS OUT OF **BULL HARBOR.** FIFTEEN DAYS BY ICEBREAKER. THEN BY SNOW TRACTOR...

"FINALLY... CROSSING THE HEISENVALD RIDGE ON FOOT.

"THE TOP OF THE WORLD. SO SILENT. SO EMPTY.

"AND THERE... RIGHT WHERE THE CAVENDISH BOYS SAID IT WOULD BE. RIGHT WHERE **NINE GENERATIONS** OF THEIR FAMILY WERE **SURE** IT WOULD BE...

"NINE GENERATIONS WHO **DIED** TRYING TO REACH THE SPOT ON WHICH WE STOOD...

"INSIDE... DARK. SILENT. LIKE THE AGE OF ALL THE WORLD WAS **CRAMMED** INTO THAT NARROW SPACE.

"THE RUINS. FROZEN. OLDER THAN THE TEMPLE AT YANG KOR...

"AND THERE, SQUATTING IN THE DARKNESS, PART OF THE DARKNESS, PART OF THE SILENCE, THE AGE..."

"AND SEATED IN FRONT OF IT, SURROUNDED BY IT, ALMOST AS THOUGH IT WERE *PART* OF IT..."

"YOU REMEMBER... I SHOWED YOU PICTURES OF THE STATUES FOUND ON KOFU IN THE THIRTIES. IT WAS LIKE THEM, BUT *BIGGER.* A HUNDRED TIMES BIGGER."

"HUMAN IN FORM COLD. FROZEN. SUCH EXQUISITE *DETAIL* IN THE *CARVING.*"

"ALMOST LIKE SOMETHING..."

"...ALIVE..."

AND WHEN I GET ANGRY I SOMETIMES DO *STUPID* THINGS.

THINGS LIKE CHARGING *HEADLONG* INTO A *PITCH BLACK ROOM.*

I'M *TOUGHER* AND *STRONGER* THAN ANY HUMAN...

...BUT I CAN'T *SEE* ANY BETTER IN THE *DARK.*

I WISH I COULD.

OOF!

GACK!

AND MY FROG-FACED FRIEND IS COMING BACK TO *FINISH* THE JOB!

HE'S FAST, BUT THIS TIME I'M *FASTER.*

IT'S NOT MY *FLESH AND BLOOD* ARM HE GETS A *HOLD* ON.

I LET HIM GET A *TASTE* OF MY *RIGHT* HAND.

THE HAND THE BEST SCIENTISTS OF THE LAST HALF CENTURY HAVE *TRIED* AND *FAILED* TO *ANALYZE.*

THEY COULDN'T FIND OUT *ANYTHING...*

...BUT AT LEAST I KNOW *ONE THING* ABOUT IT.

IT DOESN'T FEEL *PAIN.*

WONDER IF *FROGGY* DOES?

AT A GUESS, I'D SAY *YES.*

AT LEAST, *SOMETHING'S* MADE HIM CHANGE HIS *ATTITUDE* ALL OF A SUDDEN.

HE STAGGERS AROUND A BIT, LIKE HE'S TRYING TO DECIDE WHAT TO DO *NEXT.*

I DECIDE TO HELP HIM MAKE UP HIS MIND.

FEELING IS CREEPING BACK INTO MY LEFT HAND.

MOSTLY IT'S THE *WORST* PAIN I'VE EVER FELT--AND I'VE BEEN *HURT* BY *EXPERTS*--

--BUT FEELING THAT ALSO LETS ME GRAB AND HOLD THE PISTOL THE *TORCH OF LIBERTY* GAVE ME.

I DON'T KNOW *WHO* FROGGY IS, OR *WHERE* HE CAME FROM...

...BUT HE OBVIOUSLY KNOWS A *GUN* WHEN HE SEES ONE.

HE *BOLTS* FOR THE CLOSEST WINDOW.

IT HAPPENS TO BE THE *BATHROOM.*

AND I'M GOING TO LET HIM GET OUTSIDE?

LIKE *HELL!!*

VON KRUPT, KLAUS WERNER
(Photo taken 12/2/45) Committed to Eisenvalt Sanitarium. Died 6 months later. Body discovered to be infested with beetles of unknown species. No explanation.

To the best determination of the assigned investigative team, "Ragna Rok" was one of Hitler's many "Doomsday" projects initiated in the closing days of World War Two.

Principally there were known to be five individuals (see photos below) involved at key steps of the project, and so far as has been determined all five were present in the final moments. The project was apparently headed by General Klaus Werner von Krupt (see addendum under photo.)

The culmination of several years' work by the individuals, the ritual performed on Tarmagant Island (see map, pg. 162) on 23 Dec. 1944 corresponds precisely with the manifestation of the creature now code named "Hellboy" (see File #25891), the so-called "HELLBOY INCIDENT."

Professor Trevor Bruttenholm and his staff have examined both "Hellboy" and the site on Tarmagant Island extensively, and although no physical evidence can be found to link the events it seems unlikely their temporal juxtaposition is merely a coincidence.

Leopold Kurtz
(b 10/11/15)
whereabouts unknown

Ilsa Haupstein
(b 6/7/19)
whereabouts unknown

Professor Doctor Karl
Ruprect Kroenen
(b unknown)
whereabouts unknown

Name Unknown
(b unknown)
whereabouts unknown

FROGS

Frogs, like snakes, scorpions, ravens, and black cats, are traditionally considered harbingers of doom, witnessed by the following tale.

AN AFRICAN MYTH ABOUT A FROG

ON A DAY when little water was to be found, Man spent awhile in thought and realized that he might one day die, never to rise again. Man sent Dog to God to ask that he might come back to life again, like the flowering plant, after death.

Dog went off and followed his nose toward God. He was soon distracted by the smell of soup, and followed his hunger toward the source. Leaning close to watch it boil, Dog was content and forgot his mission.

Seeing that Dog was lost, Frog took it upon himself to go to God and tell him that Man did not want to live again. If Man were to be reborn, thought Frog, he would soon muddy the rivers and destroy the birthplaces of frogs.

Dog finally arrived to tell God Man's message. Leaning low, he crooned Man's need for rebirth in the song of his howl. God was touched by the devotion of Dog for Man.

But God granted the frog's wish, because he got there first.

CHAPTER TWO

I DID MY HOMEWORK BEFORE WE CAME OUT HERE.

THE HOUSE IS CALLED *CAVENDISH HALL*. IT WAS BUILT ABOUT A HUNDRED AND FIFTY YEARS AGO BY THE FIRST OF THE CAVENDISH FAMILY TO COME TO AMERICA.

BACK THEN IT STOOD ON A HIGH PROMONTORY COMMANDING A WIDE VIEW OF THE LAKE AND ALL THE LAND AROUND AS FAR AS THE HORIZON.

THESE DAYS IT'S WELL ON ITS WAY TO HAVING A SWIMMING POOL FOR A BASEMENT. IT'S BEEN SINKING SINCE THE DAY IT WAS FINISHED.

OH. DID I MENTION THERE'S SUPPOSED TO BE A *CURSE* ON THE PLACE? NOT THE HOUSE ITSELF. THE LAND. THE LAKE.

THE LOCAL INDIANS KEPT WELL CLEAR OF THIS AREA FOR A COUPLE OF THOUSAND YEARS BEFORE THE CAVENDISH FAMILY ARRIVED.

YOU MAY THINK CURSES ARE JUST SO MUCH EYEWASH, BUT I DON'T. I'VE SEEN TOO MUCH THAT MAKES ME THINK OTHERWISE.

WAY TOO MUCH.

THE EXPEDITIONS. NINE GENERATIONS OF THE CAVENDISH FAMILY BELIEVED THERE WAS *SOMETHING* AT THE TOP OF THE WORLD.

I DON'T KNOW HOW MANY OF THEM *DIED* TRYING TO FIND IT. BUT THE LAST TIME THEY TOOK *TREVOR BRUTTEN-HOLM* WITH THEM.

THE MAN I CALLED MY FATHER.

AND NOW HE'S DEAD.

AND... YOU DON'T KNOW ANYTHING ABOUT... *FROGS..?*

HELL-BOY...

QUITE ALL RIGHT, MY DEAR. I DON'T MIND *DIRECT QUESTIONS*, EVEN WHEN I DON'T *UNDER-STAND* THEM.

YOUR *SONS*, THEN.

YOU HEARD *NOTHING* FROM THEM AFTER THE EXPEDITION LEFT *BULL HARBOR?*

NO, NOTHING WAS HEARD OF *ANY* OF THEM AFTER THEY LEFT THE *BASE CAMP.*

ANOTHER *SEVENTEEN LIVES* ON THE LEDGER OF THE CAVENDISH FAMILY.

BUT... EXCUSE ME, DR. SAPIEN, ARE YOU *SURE* YOU WOULDN'T LIKE MY MAN TO TAKE YOUR HAT AND COAT?

IF I MAY *SAY*, YOU LOOK... *PALE* AND *UNWELL.*

NO, MA'AM, I'M *FINE*, THANK YOU.

DR. SAPIEN DOESN'T CARE MUCH FOR *TRAVELING.*

NOW, SINCE YOU SAY YOU DON'T MIND *DIRECT QUESTIONS*, I HAVE A COUPLE. SUCH AS, *NINE GENERATIONS* SEEMS AN AWFULLY *LONG* TIME FOR A FAMILY OBSESSION...

DOES IT? I REALLY WOULDN'T KNOW.

IT HAS ALWAYS SEEMED PERFECTLY *NATURAL* TO ME. IN ALL MY LIFE I HAVE NEVER KNOWN ANY OTHER WAY.

OUR FAMILY FORTUNE WAS FOUND-ED IN EUROPE, BY *ELIHU CAVENDISH.* HE BEGAN AS A SIMPLE *WHALER.* BY THE TIME HE *DIED,* HE HAD BEEN *MASTER* OF MANY GREAT SHIPS.

"BUT HE WAS NEVER AT REST, NEVER *SATISFIED.*

"HIS TRAVELS HAD TAKEN HIM AROUND THE WORLD AND BACK TWO DOZEN TIMES.

"IN STRANGE PORTS HE LEARNED... STRANGE THINGS. "

FINALLY HIS TRAVELS BROUGHT HIM TO AMERICA, AND HERE HE BUILT THIS HOUSE. THIS *CURSED* HOUSE.

HE CHOSE THIS LOCATION WITH GREAT *CARE.* NO ONE KNOWS *WHY.*

"WITH THE HOUSE COMPLET-ED, HE SET ABOUT PREPAR-ING AN EXPEDITION TO THE FARTHEST REACHES OF THE ARCTIC. TO SEARCH FOR SOMETHING. SOMETHING HE LEARNED OF FROM A SCRAP OF ANCIENT PARCHMENT HE HAD ACQUIRED IN SOME LOST CORNER OF THE WORLD.

"BEFORE HE COULD LEAVE HE DIED OF TYPHUS. HE WAS ONE OF *THOUSANDS* WHO DIED THAT YEAR. "

AS MUCH AS ANYWHERE ELSE, I SUPPOSE THAT IS WHERE OUR CURSE WAS BEGUN. ELIHU CAVENDISH'S UNFULFILLED QUEST HAS HAUNTED EVERY MALE OF THE FAMILY EVER SINCE.

FOR NINE GENERATIONS, ALMOST TWO HUNDRED YEARS, EACH PROUD YOUNG MAN HAS SAILED OFF TO FIND... I DON'T KNOW WHAT. A DREAM. A MYTH.

"NOW MY SONS HAVE GONE. MY THREE BOYS. I PRAYED THEY WOULD BE SPARED THIS, BUT MY PRAYERS WENT UNANSWERED.

"AND SO, PERHAPS, THE CURSE ENDS. MY SONS HAD NO SONS OF THEIR OWN. IF THEY ARE DEAD--AND I FEAR THEY MUST BE--THE CAVENDISH LINE DIES WITH THEM.

"AND SOON, VERY SOON, I WILL DIE, AND THIS HORRID OLD HOUSE WILL SINK AT LAST INTO THE BLACK WATERS OF THE LAKE...

"...AND BE HIDDEN FOREVER FROM THE EYES OF GOD."

WE'RE... VERY SORRY, MA'AM.

TIME FOR YOU TO GET WET!

AND NOT A MOMENT TOO SOON! THIS BEARD WAS STARTING TO MAKE ME FEEL CLAUSTROPHOBIC.

I COULD REALLY USE A SWIM!

ABE.

I WISH I COULD TELL YOU ABOUT ABE. THAT'S NOT HIS REAL NAME, OF COURSE. "ABRAHAM SAPIEN" IS A BIT OF A BAD JOKE.

HE WAS DISCOVERED WHEN PLUMBERS WORKING IN THE BASEMENT OF ST. TRINIAN'S HOSPITAL IN WASHINGTON, D.C., BROKE OPEN A SEALED DOOR AND DISCOVERED A LONG-FORGOTTEN CHAMBER.

ICTHYO SAPIEN

· APRIL 14 1865

THE BUREAU TOOK HIS NAME FROM THE INSCRIPTION ON A SCRAP OF PAPER PINNED UP NEAR THE TUBE... THE DAY PRESIDENT LINCOLN DIED.

UNFORTUNATELY, IT SEEMS MY FROGGY FRIEND IS TOUGH ENOUGH TO *TAKE* WHATEVER I HAND OUT.

I BOUNCE OFF THE VAULTED CEILING LIKE A SACK OF WET CEMENT.

A PIECE OF MY BRAIN REGISTERS THE *DAMAGE* TO THE FINE OLD ARCHITECTURE.

IT'S MY LAST *CALM* THOUGHT FOR A WHILE.

I LAND ON MY FEET.

AND I LAND *MAD.*

KRAK

IF THERE'S ANYTHING LEFT IN YOU THAT CAN STILL TALK, **START NOW**.

LAST CHANCE.

NO?

KRASH

WELL...

...THAT'S *ALL* FOR YOU!

IT NOW SEEMS UNLIKELY I WILL DISCOVER ANYTHING OF LIZ'S WHEREABOUTS FROM THE TRANSFORMED BUTLER.

AND JUST ABOUT THEN I REALIZE ABE HAS BEEN GONE WAY TOO LONG...

HELLBOY WAS RIGHT ABOUT THE FOUNDATION. I FOUND A WAY THROUGH EASILY. IT'S AMAZING THE OLD HOUSE IS STILL STANDING, THE LOWER WALLS ARE SO FULL OF HOLES.

THE WATER IS DARKER THAN ANY I'VE EVER SWUM IN BE-FORE. IT SEEMS ALMOST TO *CLING* TO MY SKIN, LIKE INK, LIKE OIL.

AND THERE IS NOTHING AT ALL *ALIVE* DOWN HERE. NO *ANIMALS.* NO *FISH.* NOT EVEN *ALGAE.*

A PLACE OF *DEATH.*

OLD DEATH.

AND AS I REACH THE SURFACE, I BEGIN TO THINK...

CHAPTER THREE

WHEN I LOOK BACK ON ALL THE YEARS OF MY CAREER AS THE WORLD'S GREATEST PARANORMAL INVESTIGATOR, IT SEEMS AS THOUGH I'VE SPENT A LOT OF TIME WITH BOTH FEET OFF THE GROUND.

LEAPING, FALLING, SOMETIMES BEING PICKED UP AND HURLED, I'VE SORT OF GOTTEN USED TO IT, IN FACT.

BUT THIS IS DIFFERENT. I WAS PULLED DOWN THROUGH THE FLOOR OF THE OLD *CAVENDISH* MANSION, AND IT SEEMS NOW LIKE THAT WAS HOURS AGO. DAYS AGO.

I HIT WATER AND THE PIECE OF MY BRAIN THAT'S STILL WORKING TELLS ME THAT MEANS I CAN'T HAVE FALLEN NEARLY AS FAR AS IT SEEMED.

THE CAVENDISH HOUSE SITS ON A SHALLOW SPIT OF LAND STICKING OUT INTO A LAKE. IT'S ALMOST AT THE SAME LEVEL AS THE WATER.

THE LAKE IS ONLY A FEW DOZEN FEET ABOVE SEA LEVEL, AND SINCE NO WATER CAN BE LOWER THAN SEA LEVEL

...THIS BIG, DARK, COLD POOL CAN'T BE MORE THAN FIFTY OR SIXTY FEET BELOW THE HOUSE.

AS ALL THIS RUNS THROUGH MY MIND I CAN ALMOST HEAR *LIZ* CHIDING ME.

"COME ON, MR. WIZARD," SHE'D SAY, "THERE'S WORK TO BE DONE."

BUT I DON'T REALLY HEAR HER, LIZ IS GONE, SNATCHED FROM HER ROOM BY SOME UNKNOWN FORCE.

THE SAME FORCE, I'D BET, THAT PULLED ME DOWN HERE.

IT FEELS *BAD* DOWN HERE. ALL OVER MY BODY COARSE, BLACK LITTLE HAIRS RISE AND BRISTLE AT THE TOUCH OF *EVIL*.

AND THEN I HEAR THE VOICE, THE STRANGE, *FAMILIAR* VOICE...

WHAT YOU FEEL, CREATURE, IS THE LONG AND *BLOODY* HISTORY OF THIS PLACE.

OPEN YOUR SMALL MIND TO IT. CAN YOU HEAR THE *SCREAMS* OF FUTILE SACRIFICE? CAN YOU SMELL THE HOT BLOOD ON THESE COLD STONES?

EIGHT HUNDRED YEARS AGO MEN STILL WORSHIPPED THE *SERPENT* AND SOUGHT TO APPEASE HIM WITH THE BLOOD OF INNOCENTS.

FOOLS!

EIGHT CENTURIES AGO MORTALS LACKED THE *POWER* TO FREE THE BEAST.

BUT THAT POWER EXISTS NOW, HERE,

IN *ME!*

THE SERPENT CARES NOT FOR THE BLOOD OF MEN. HE CRAVES BUT ONE THING, AND THAT IS *FREEDOM*.

HE DOESN'T UTTER SO MUCH AS A *SQUEAK*, BUT THE *AIR* RINGS LIKE SOME GREAT FROZEN BELL...

...AND I FEEL FOR ALL THE WORLD LIKE SOMEBODY JUST SWATTED ME WITH A SUBMARINE.

I HIT HARD, HARD ENOUGH TO KNOCK THE WIND OUT OF EVEN ME.

NEVER AGAIN RAISE A HAND TO ME, CREATURE.

I *CONJURED* YOU INTO THIS WORLD, AND I CAN *WIPE* YOU FROM IT.

I'M BEGINNING TO BELIEVE HIM.

I'VE BEEN A PARANORMAL INVESTIGATOR GETTING ON FORTY YEARS NOW. I'VE SEEN A LOT OF THINGS. LEARNED A LOT OF THINGS.

THE POCKETS OF MY OLD COAT ARE FULL OF CHARMS AND TALISMANS I'VE COLLECTED FROM THE FOUR CORNERS OF THE WORLD.

BY RIGHTS ANY ONE OF THEM SHOULD HAVE PROTECTED ME FROM JUST ABOUT ANYTHING.

BUT EITHER HE'S *NEUTRALIZED* ALL OF THEM SOMEHOW OR--WORSE--HE'S JUST TOO DAMN POWERFUL FOR THEM TO WORK AGAINST HIM.

NICE TRICK, PUTTING YOUR HEAD BACK TOGETHER.

UNTIL I KNOW *WHICH*, I DECIDE TO *STALL* THINGS A LITTLE BIT.

I WAS UNEASY FROM THE MOMENT I CAME INTO THIS PLACE.

THE MORE MY EYES BECOME ACCUSTOMED TO THE GLOOM, THE MORE I SEE MY DISQUIETUDE WAS NOT WITHOUT CAUSE,

FLED INTO DARKNESS TO WALLOW IN THE DRY DUST OF THEIR LOST GENERATIONS.

THIS IS A PLACE OF THE DEAD...

...BUT IT IS NOT A QUIET PLACE.

THE UNMISTAKABLE IMPRESSION IS THAT SOMETHING HAS BEEN... ROOTING AROUND IN THE REMAINS.

...AND IF GOD CHOOSE
I SHALL BUT LOVE THEE BETTER
AFTER DEATH

AND HERE, PERHAPS, I'VE FOUND THE *CULPRITS*.

THIS PLACE OF DEATH IS NOT *ENTIRELY* WITHOUT LIFE.

SOME HOPE.

ENOUGH, OLAFSEN. WE DO NOT WANT THE CREATURE *DEAD.*

HE WOULD BE OF *LITTLE* USE THAT WAY.

. . . .

YES? YOU HAVE SOMETHING TO SAY?

...WHO..?

...HOW..?

YES... PERHAPS IT IS TIME I TOLD YOU SOMETHING *MORE* OF MYSELF.

FOLLOWING THE... EXAGGERATED REPORTS OF MY DEATH, I LEFT THE BLESSED SOIL OF RUSSIA.

I KNEW A TOWN IN ITALY, SMALL, SECLUDED. A PLACE I COULD *REST.* A PLACE I COULD *REGATHER* MY POWER.

FOR MORE THAN TWENTY YEARS I LIVED IN ISOLATION, PREACHING ON OCCASION TO THOSE BRAVE SOULS WHO DARED APPROACH ME.

TELLING OF THE COMING RAGNA ROK, THE NEW AGE OF THE SERPENT. SPEAKING AS THE *PROPHET* OF THE APOCALYPSE.

BUT MOSTLY, MOSTLY WRAPPED IN *SILENCE* AS I LISTEN FOR THE VOICES THAT HAD SPOKEN TO ME UNDER THE RIVER.

LISTENED...

...AND HEARD NOTHING.

A SIGN THAT CAME AT LAST IN THE FORM OF A SMALL AND CRINGING HUMAN.

HIS NAME WAS *HIMMLER,* AND HE CAME TO *HIRE* ME.

TO TAKE ME TO THAT LAND WHICH WAS THE ANCIENT *ENEMY* OF MY BELOVED RUSSIA...

TO TAKE ME TO *GERMANY.*

SO I WAITED INSTEAD FOR SOME OTHER KIND OF *COMMUNICATION.* I WAITED FOR A *SIGN.*

THERE I WAS INTRODUCED TO A SMALL, DOOMED MADMAN.

BUT A MADMAN IN WHOSE DOOM I SAW A CHANCE TO HARNESS *UNLIMITED RESOURCES.*

I PERMITTED MYSELF TO BE JOINED WITH THOSE PUNY MINDS THE *REICH* HAD ASSEMBLED FOR ITSELF, BELIEVING THEM *UNEQUALED* IN THE WORLD, UNEQUALED IN THEIR TALENTS FOR CREATING WEAPONS OF *MASS DESTRUCTION.*

THEY WERE FOOLS, OF COURSE, COMPARED TO ME, BUT I SAW IN THEM ROUGH GEMS I MIGHT SHAPE AND POLISH, CRUDE THEIR THOUGHTS AND MINDS MIGHT BE...

...BUT ALSO UTTERLY *UNTARNISHED* BY THE LIMITATIONS OF *CONSCIENCE* AND *MORALITY.*

I WORKED CLOSELY WITH THE THREE I DEEMED MOST *RATIONAL* AMONG THEM. I GUIDED THEM, SO THAT IN TIME THEY THOUGHT THEY HAD THEMSELVES CONCEIVED THE PROJECT THEY NAMED *RAGNA ROK,*

HAD THEMSELVES *IMAGINED* THE CONSTRUCTION OF THE *RAGNA ROK ENGINE,*

BEHIND THEIR BACKS I *LAUGHED* AT THEIR RIDICULOUS CONCEITS. NO MERE HUMAN MIND COULD EVEN HAVE CONCEIVED SUCH A WONDROUS DEVICE, AS NO MERE HUMAN FORM COULD CONTAIN THE FORCES WHICH THE ENGINE WOULD SUMMON, MAGNIFY AND DIRECT.

DIRECT INTO *ME,* SO THAT I MIGHT BECOME THE *KEY* BY WHICH THE BEAST WOULD BE AT LAST RELEASED FROM THEIR PRIMEVAL PRISON.

AS THE THOUSAND-YEAR REICH GROUND DOWN TO ITS LAST, BITTER, BLOODY DAYS, THE PROJECT NEARED ITS CULMINATION.

ASTROLOGY GUIDED ME TO THE *PLACE*.

NUMEROLOGY GUIDED ME TO THE *TIME*.

THERE WAS NO MEANS BY WHICH THE *RESULT* OF THE EXPERIMENT COULD BE ACCURATELY PREDICTED.

THE NAZIS THOUGHT IT *FAILED*.

I KNEW BETTER.

I DID NOT KNOW PRECISELY *WHAT*, BUT I KNEW *SOMETHING* HAD BEEN CONJURED FORTH FROM THE WORLDS BEYOND.

YOU.

BUT BEFORE I COULD PRESS MY INVESTIGATION FURTHER, THE TIDE OF WAR TURNED IRREVOCABLY.

GERMANY WAS DESTROYED. HITLER, HIMMLER, ALL THE REST WERE *DEAD*.

AS TRIUMPHANT FOREIGN ARMIES MARCHED OVER THE ASHES OF THE FATHERLAND, MY BRAVE ASSOCIATES FLED TO PREARRANGED HIDING PLACES.

I WAS *ALONE*.

AND FOR THE *FIRST TIME*... I WAS *UNSURE*.

AND IT WAS THEN, AS IF MY MOMENTARY WEAKNESS HAD SOMEHOW REKINDLED THEM...

...THAT I HEARD ONCE MORE THE LONG SILENT *VOICES*.

THEY SPOKE, AND THEY BADE ME *GO*,

THEY BADE ME GO *NORTH*.

NORTH, TO THE ARCTIC WASTES.

TO THE VERY *TOP* OF THE *WORLD*.

WITH A HANDFUL OF PAID COMPANIONS, I MARCHED UP OVER THE BROAD SHOULDER OF THE WORLD, NORTH AND EVER NORTH.

THOSE WHO MARCHED WITH ME HAD NO INTEREST IN MY MISSION. THEY CAME ONLY FOR THE *GOLD* I PROMISED.

THEIR SOULS WERE SMALL, BUT THEY WERE SUFFICIENT TO SUSTAIN ME.

SO IT WAS *ALONE* THAT I ARRIVED AT LAST AT MY DESTINATION.

SO IT WAS MY EYES ALONE WHICH LOOKED UPON THE FABLED TEMPLE OF THE *OGDRU-JAHAD*, BUILT UNCOUNTED EONS PAST BY THE FIRST RACE OF MEN.

AND *WITHIN* ITS FROZEN WALLS, SOMETHING OLDER STILL, FOR THE TEMPLE WAS BUILT TO *CONTAIN* IT.

THE *SADU-HEM*, LEFT BY THE OGDRU-JAHAD THAT THEY MIGHT ALWAYS HAVE A FOOTHOLD IN THE WORLD FROM WHICH THEY WERE FOREVER BANISHED.

HIDDEN FROM THE EYES OF GOD, DEAD AND FOSSILIZED, TO ANOTHER IT WOULD HAVE SEEMED BUT A GROTESQUE STATUE.

BUT NOT TO ME.

I FELT ITS MIND, ALIVE AND WAITING.

SEATING MYSELF AT THE FOOT OF THE LIVING STATUE, I SENT MY BODY INTO A TRANCE, THAT MY MIND MIGHT REACH OUT TO THE SHADOW OF LIFE DEEP WITHIN ITS STONY COILS.

THROUGH THE ANCIENT SLUMBER I PENETRATED, AND SAW AS IF WITH THE SADU-HEM'S OWN EYES THE **VOID**...

...AND THE IMPRISONED FORMS OF THE SEVEN BEASTS...

NUNN-JAHAD

ADAD-JAHAD

AMON-JAHAD

IRRA-JAHAD

BELILI-JAHAD

NERGAL-JAHAD

NAMRAT-JAHAD

WRAPPED THEY WERE IN **DARKNESS** AND **DREAMING**, AND IN THAT SILENT STATE I **JOINED** THEM.

SO DID THE LONG YEARS PASS, TIMELESS, ETERNAL, SEEMING AS A MOMENT, SEEMING AS A CENTURY.

UNTIL THE TOUCH OF A HUMAN HAND **AWAKENED** ME.

I SAW **YOU**, CREATURE, AND KNEW YOU CALLED THIS MAN YOUR "FATHER."

THE HAND OF THE MAN NAMED **TREVOR BRUTTENHOLM**. AND IN THE INSTANT OF OUR CONTACT I SAW ALL THERE WAS TO SEE WITHIN HIS FRAIL, MORTAL MIND.

AFTER HIS LONG SLEEP SADU-HEM WAS **HUNGRY**, BUT I BADE HIM **SPARE** THESE MORTALS FOR A WHILE.

I SAW IN THEM A GREATER USE AS NEW **DISCIPLES** TO MY PLAN, THAN AS A QUICK RESPITE OF HUNGER TO AN ANCIENT GODLING.

YOU WILL APPRECIATE HOW **IMPORTANT** IS MY PLAN, WHEN I TELL YOU SADU-HEM AGREED.

BUT THEY WERE NOT ENOUGH. WITH THE POWER THAT HAD GROWN IN ME DURING MY LONG STILLNESS I REACHED OUT.

I SOUGHT WITH MY MIND THE OTHER HUMANS, THE BASE CAMP I HAD SEEN IN THE MEMORIES OF BRUTTENHOLM.

HE LET THE HUMANS LIVE, TO BE **VESSELS** FOR THE SEED OF THE GREAT SERPENT.

I TOUCHED THE OTHERS, AND I SUMMONED THEM TO ME.

I NEEDED THEM, YOU SEE, AS **SLAVE LABOR**, TO LIFT AND BEAR SADU-HEM ACROSS THE ICE, DOWN THE SLOPE OF THE WORLD TO THE BOAT.

ONCE HE WAS **ENSCONCED** WITHIN THAT METAL WOMB I LET HIM FEED AT LAST ON THE MEMBERS OF THE EXPEDITION.

ALL SAVE BRUTTENHOLM, WHOM I ALLOWED TO ESCAPE, ONCE WE REACHED NEW YORK.

I KNEW HIS FIRST CONSCIOUS ACTION WOULD BE TO CONTACT YOU, THE ONE HE CALLED "HELLBOY."

IN THE MEANTIME, I WAITED, WAITED WHILE THE POWER WITH-IN ME GREW AND **STRENGTHENED.**

AT LAST MY **PATIENCE** WAS **DOUBLY** REWARDED. **YOU** ARRIVED...

...AND WITH YOU CAME AN **UNANTICIPATED BONUS.**

AN **EXTRA** SOURCE OF POWER WITH WHICH I NOW **EXPUNGE** ALL FURTHER DELAY, THE TIME OF **RAGNA ROK** IS **HERE**

LIZ!

CHAPTER FOUR

IT *MULTIPLIES* MY OWN POWER, AND THUS LINKED *BOTH* FLOW INTO *SADU-HEM.*

AND OUT OF *HIM* IT WILL GO INTO THE ETERNAL *VOID,* THE *ABYSS,* THERE TO *SMITE* THE ANCIENT PRISON OF *SERPENT.*

THE BINDING PLACE SHALL BE FOREVER *BROKEN.*

THE *OGDRU-JAHAD* ONCE MORE SHALL *RULE* THE WORLD!

WHAT A *PITY* YOU CHOSE TO STAND *AGAINST* ME, CREATURE.

MY CONJURER'S SKILL SUMMONED YOU INTO THIS WORLD HALF A CENTURY AGO, SOLELY THAT YOU MIGHT BE A *PART* OF THIS GREAT MOMENT.

THAT YOU MIGHT BE THE *CONDUIT* INTO THE EVERLAST-ING DARKNESS.

BUT NOW I HAVE THE UNMATCHED POWER OF THE *WOMAN.*

YOU BECOME SIMPLY AN *ANNOYANCE.*

A PIECE OF MY BRAIN IS STILL WORKING ENOUGH TO *HEAR* THE WIZARD'S WORDS.

A *SMALLER* PIECE DOES THE BEST IT CAN TO *UNDERSTAND* THEM AS THE ICE-COLD TONGUE OF THE FROG-THING THAT WAS *SVEN OLAFSEN* SUCKS THE LIFE OUT OF ME.

ABE!

BUT...

...NOT ALONE.

IN SOME KIND OF TRANCE.

AND BEHIND HIM...

...THE SHADOWS SPEAK...

WAKE UP, GIRL

THE WIZARD **MOCKED** THE SCIENTISTS WHO TRIED TO UNDERSTAND THE POWER LOCKED UP INSIDE LIZ SHERMAN.

HE THOUGHT HE KNEW BETTER THAN THEM. THOUGHT HE COULD REACH DOWN INSIDE HER AND PULL OUT JUST AS MUCH OF THAT POWER AS HE NEEDED.

PITY.

IF HE'D ONLY **ASKED** ME, I COULD HAVE TOLD HIM HE WAS **WRONG.**

WHAT A **MESS!**

YOU'LL HAVE TO LET ME READ YOUR **REPORT** ON THIS ONE, HELLBOY...

...ASSUMING WE GET OUT SO YOU CAN **WRITE** IT.

DEAL.

THERE'S A LOT MORE
CONFIDENCE IN MY *VOICE* THAN
THERE IS IN MY *HEART*.

ALL AROUND US THE OLD
STONES OF CAVENDISH HOUSE
ARE GIVING UP THEIR LONG WAR
WITH *GRAVITY*.

STATUARY A MUSEUM CURATOR
WOULD GIVE YEARS OFF HIS LIFE
TO POSSESS RAINS DOWN INTO
THE CAULDRON THAT USED TO
BE *SADU-HEM*.

I WONDER IF THE CREATURE IS
STILL ALIVE ENOUGH TO FEEL
THE PAIN OF THE STONE AND
THE FIRE.

I HOPE
SO.

MOVE!
MOVE!!
MOVE!!!

HEY! STEPS!

GO UP! GO UP!

I... DON'T THINK I'M DONE HERE YET...

I DON'T REMEMBER TOO MUCH OF IT, HELLBOY.

I WAS LOOKING AT WHAT I THOUGHT WAS A **STATUE** OF OLD ELIHU CAVENDISH...

...AND THEN THERE WAS A **HARPOON** STICKING THROUGH A GUY...

AND THERE WAS A REALLY BIG MONSTER...

IMAGINE MY **CONFUSION.**

AND WHEN EVERYTHING CAUGHT FIRE...

I DIDN'T KNOW WHAT THE HELL WAS GOING ON!

SOUNDS TO ME LIKE OLD MAN CAVENDISH TOOK OVER YOUR BODY, ABE.

HE WAS THE ONE WHO DID THE HARPOONING.

YES, YOUR "MR. RAGNA ROK" KILLED THE **LAST** OF ELIHU'S FAMILY, AN OLD FAMILY WITH A LOT OF **PAIN** ATTACHED TO ITS NAME.

ENOUGH TO ALLOW HIM TO REACH FROM BEYOND THE GRAVE TO EXTRACT HIS **VENGEANCE.**

MM. OR MAYBE HE WAS JUST **PISSED** BECAUSE SOMEBODY ELSE FOUND THAT THING UP IN THE ARCTIC BEFORE HIS PEOPLE DID.

THEY SPENT A LONG TIME LOOKING. WE DON'T KNOW THINGS WOULD HAVE BEEN ANY DIF- FERENT IF THEY'D FOUND SADU-HEM.

WHAT ABOUT YOU, LIZ? THAT OLD WIZARD HAD YOU **ZONKED** PRETTY GOOD. DO YOU REMEMBER ANY MORE THAN ABE DOES?

A LITTLE, NOT MUCH.

WHERE THE HELL DID HE COME FROM?

Personal reminiscences by Mike Mignola.

LEFT: This is a drawing done for a convention program book — I added the name Hellboy at the last minute and it made me laugh. The name stuck and the character started to take shape in my head.

BELOW: I first envisioned *Hellboy* as a team book, but I couldn't come up with a name for any of the other characters or the team. Hellboy's in the process of mutating from that first drawing into the guy we know and love today — look at the size of his neck!

RIGHT: Hellboy in his final form. I originally intended this piece to be a promotional poster for the first *Hellboy* miniseries but I wasn't happy with Hellboy's right hand.

MORE FIRST THINGS—

THE following stories are the first Hellboy stories ever produced, done to promote the miniseries and introduce the character. The first story ran in *San Diego Comic-Con Comics #2*, given away at the 1993 San Diego Comic Con. The second story was published in the *Comics Buyer's Guide.*

I wasn't much concerned with plot, but I did learn a couple of things — Hellboy looks better with a coat, and I like to draw gorillas with big bolts sticking out of them.

The art on this page is the first Hellboy promotional piece, and the first appearance of his coat.

CURIOUS JUXTAPOSITION. I'VE BEEN AROUND THE WORLD AND BACK A FEW TIMES IN MY DAY, BUT I'VE NEVER SEEN ANYTHING QUITE LIKE **THIS**.

A BIG COWBOY BOOT. AND AN EGYPTIAN SCARAB BEETLE. AND A SWASTIKA.

TOO MANY **IDIOMS**, IF YOU ASK ME.

ONLY THERE'S NOBODY HERE TO ASK ME.

IN THE PAST COUPLE OF YEARS A WHOLE FLOCK OF SMALL TOWNS HAVE **DRIED UP** DOWN AROUND THESE PARTS.

PEOPLE VANISHED WITHOUT A TRACE. NO SIGN OF **VIOLENCE**. JUST--**GONE**.

THIS TOWN IS THE LATEST. AND THE FIRST TO COME TO MY ATTENTION.

HUH?

A DOG?

A DOG. KIND OF A MANGY LITTLE MUTT. LOOKS **HUNGRY**, TOO.

MUST HAVE BEEN HERE ON HIS OWN SINCE EVERYBODY VANISHED.

HEY, PUP! DON'T BE AFRAID.

I'M NOT NEARLY AS **SCARY** AS I...

..LOOK...

THAT SHOULDN'T HAVE **HURT** ME. I MAY NOT BE AS **SCARY** AS I LOOK, BUT I'M EVERY BIT AS **TOUGH**.

THIS MAY OR MAY NOT BE THE REAL GOD **ANUBIS**...

BUT WHOEVER HE IS, HE'S GOT A PRETTY GOOD CHANCE TO MAKE GOOD ON HIS **THREATS**.

UNLESS I DO SOMETHING **FIRST**.

MY **ACCIDENTAL** IMPACT WEAKENED THE NUTS AND BOLTS HOLDING THE GAS STATION SIGN TOGETHER.

WUNG

LET'S SEE WHAT A COUPLE OF **DELIBERATE** HITS WILL DO...

PANG

SHUCK

GWAAAAA AAAA

YEAH... MAYBE HE'S REALLY ANUBIS, BUT THE ARROW GOES INTO HIM WITH A RED, WET NOISE LIKE ANY KIND OF FLESH GETTING **SLICED**.

AND HIS **HOWL** IS LIKE THE HOWL OF ANY INJURED ANIMAL.

A VERY **POWERFUL** PUPPET.

I'M NOT SURE AT THIS POINT HOW MUCH OF THIS IS VON KLEMPT'S DIRECTION...

...AND HOW MUCH IS HIS REACTION TO THE **PAIN** OF HIS SHATTERED **HAND**.

UNFORTUNATELY, EITHER WAY I DON'T HAVE MUCH **CHOICE** IN HOW TO **DEAL** WITH HIM.

SORRY, FUZZY!

I KNOW THIS **HURTS**, SO I'LL TRY TO PUT YOU TO **SLEEP** AS **FAST** AS I CAN!

I KICK HIM AS HARD AS I CAN IN THE TWO MAIN **NERVE JUNCTIONS** JUST UNDER HIS BIG JAW.

IT'S A **DANGEROUS** MOVE. IF I'VE **MISJUDGED** HIS STRENGTH, AND HE DOESN'T GO DOWN...

HEY-- HATE TO BE THE ONE TO **BREAK** IT TO YOU, HERR HERMAN...

...BUT THAT'S WHY I'M **HERE**!

FOOLS! IMBECILES! STOP THIS SENSELESS FIGHTING!!

YOU'VE SMASHED THE LAB!

YOU'VE DESTROYED MY PRECIOUS **EQUIPMENT**.

PLEASE!

PLEASE **HELP** ME!!

THE GIRL IS STILL **ALIVE**.

THE TRANSFUSION CAN STILL BE ACCOMPLISHED.

HUH??

YOU CAN **TALK**??

MAYBE IT'S SOME KIND OF NAZI **VENTRILOQUISM,** OR MAYBE I HADN'T BEEN GIVEN THE STRAIGHT **DOPE** ON BRUTUS.

SHOOMP

BZZZZ

EITHER WAY, I KNOW RIGHT OFF I DON'T WANT TO HEAR THAT **VOICE** AGAIN...

YOU **DID** IT! YOU **DESTROYED** THEM **BOTH!**

YEAH. SURE. WELL, THAT WAS THE **PLAN,** RIGHT?

NEXT TIME, HELL-BOY!

NEXT TIME YOU **DIE!!**

YEAH, MAYBE THAT'S WHAT HE SAYS. OR MAYBE IT'S JUST 'ARRGH...,' I'M NOT IN MUCH OF A MOOD TO FIND OUT.

SO THE DAMSEL AND I STAND A WHILE AND WATCH THE CASTLE **BURN.** SURE MAKES A MERRY BLAZE FOR SOMETHING BUILT MOSTLY OF **STONE.**

SHE LEANS UP AGAINST ME AND **SIGHS** KIND OF CONTENTEDLY...

MIKE MIGNOLA
IT WAS ALL HIS IDEA

JOHN BYRNE
ALONG FOR THE RIDE

...SO OF COURSE THERE'S **NO WAY** I'M GONNA TELL HER I HAD **NO IDEA** TOSSING VON KLEMPT AT BRUTUS WAS THE WAY TO **WIN...**

HELLBOY™

GALLERY

featuring

SIMON BISLEY
colored by Matthew Hollingsworth

MIKE ALLRED

ART ADAMS
colored by Matthew Hollingsworth

FRANK MILLER

FRED BLANCHARD

and

GARY GIANNI

HELLBOY
Mike Mignola
SEED OF DESTRUCTION
with John Byrne
128-page color paperback
ISBN: 1-56971-316-2 $17.95
WAKE THE DEVIL
144-page color paperback
ISBN: 1-56971-226-3 $17.95
THE CHAINED COFFIN AND OTHERS
168-page color paperback
ISBN: 1-56971-349-9 $17.95
THE LOST ARMY
Written by Christopher Golden
200-page B&W paperback
ISBN: 1-56971-185-2 $14.95

ZOMBIEWORLD
CHAMPION OF THE WORMS
Mike Mignola & Pat McEown
80-page color paperback
ISBN: 1-56971-334-0 $8.95

ART ADAMS'
CREATURE FEATURES
Arthur Adams
104-page color paperback
ISBN: 1-56971-214-X $13.95

SERGIO ARAGONÉS'
LOUDER THAN WORDS
Sergio Aragonés
160-page B&W paperback
ISBN: 1-56971-343-X $12.95

BIG GUY AND RUSTY THE BOY ROBOT
Frank Miller & Geof Darrow
80-page color paperback
ISBN: 1-56971-201-8 $14.95

CONCRETE
THINK LIKE A MOUNTAIN
Paul Chadwick
160-page color paperback
ISBN: 1-56971-176-3 $17.95

ELRIC: STORMBRINGER
Michael Moorcock & P. Craig Russell
232-page color paperback
ISBN:1-56971-336-7 $17.95

FAX FROM SARAJEVO
Joe Kubert
208-page color paperback
ISBN: 1-56971-346-4 $16.95

THE HAMMER
ONE BIG LIE
Kelley Jones
120-page color paperback
ISBN: 1-56971-340-5 $12.95

HARD BOILED
Frank Miller & Geof Darrow
128-page color paperback
ISBN: 1-878574-58-2 $15.95

MADMAN COMICS
Michael Allred
VOLUME TWO
160-page color paperback
ISBN: 1-56971-186-0 $17.95

MONKEYMAN & O'BRIEN
Arthur Adams
136-page color paperback
ISBN: 1-56971-232-8 $16.95

RASCALS IN PARADISE
Jim Silke
104-page color paperback
ISBN: 1-56971-075-9 $16.95

SIN CITY
Frank Miller
SIN CITY
208-page B&W paperback
ISBN: 1-878574-59-0 $15.00
FAMILY VALUES
128-page B&W paperback
ISBN: 1-56971-313-8 $10.00